Short Sleeves

– A Book for Friends –

™

H. T. Manogue

Short Sleeves

A Book For Friends

ISBN 0-9778130-0-2

Shortsleeves.net

To:

Freedom
Awareness
Connection
&
Contrast

™

My Special Thanks

For your help and support:

Brandon Jones
Leah Jones
Harlan Whitley
Kim Leonard
Joanie Hatch
Elliot Manogue
Megan Manogue

Note From The Author:

This work was started in spring 2005 and completed in January 2006.

It is the first in a series. The 2007 Collection is in progress.

I have so many people to thank for the genesis of this book.

My poetic inspirations: Rumi, Rilke Goethe, Blake, Dickinson, Ikemoto, Dogen, Lao-Tsu.

All the thinkers and pioneers who open doors with questions about life and how it should be lived. Even though their language and time portals are different, the message is not:

Love of self, brings about love of all.

And to all religions for being the catalyst to search and try to understand more about who we are and why we are in this time/ space wonderland.

I dedicate this book to them and to all who read these words. Somewhere in these pages a spark could ignite you to look at yourself and smile...H.T.M.

P.S. - And especially to Mom and Dad!

Table Of Contents

You Are The Secret Of God's Secret

You Are The Mirror Of Divine Beauty.

Everything In The Universe Is Within You

Ask All From Yourself.

The One At Whom You Are Looking Is

Also You...

Rumi

Spirit

Spirit Find Me   Where You Left Me

Covered In A Cloud

My Mind Sits In Questions

Watching Stars Go Round

Maybe I Should Find Thee

Waiting For A Ride   Back To The Beginning

When Mind Had No Time

Spirit   I Can Feel You

Just A Vibe Apart

Meeting Will Be Heaven

And Another Start

To: Our Inner Guide

Life In Line

Rocks Moving Thru Time

Changing Energies In Our Minds

Brings Us Closer

To

Life In Line

To: New Creation

Prayer

Point Of Mind   No Where Time

Give Me Power   Any Hour

Dot The Line   In My Mind

Along The Way

Wide Open Point Of Time

Think I

Need Some Overtime

Creative Star

Place Of Understanding

Needs No Form

It's Moment Living And Joyous Giving

Creative Star Our Beauty Bar

Resting Brightly In Our Jar

It's Not Far

And Is

Who You Are

To: Your Creation

Farm To Be

Release Me

Put Me In The Sea

Swimming Trouble Free   In Vibration Glee

Life To Me   Super Connection Tree

Fruit Of Thee And Me

My Farm To Be

To: Higher Vibrations

Time Frame

A Moments Creation

High Speed   Expansion Brain

There You Are

Within Me   Can It Be

You And Me   Question Free

Follow That Star   That You Are

Our Inner Voice   Is The Choice

Freedom Gain   There Is No Pain

Life In Your Time Frame

To: Focused Moments

Faith

Misty Glow of Light

In The Shadows Of Questions

Clear My Mind With Faith

To: Prayer

Love Now

It's Your Dime   Grab A Time

Love Now   You Know How

Make Your Self   Wow The Now

Creative Mac   Your Voice Will Act

Magical Now   Is A Reborn Trowel

Could Be A Poetry Owl

Open Door   There Is No Score

Love's In Line   It's About Your Time

To: Love Of Self-First

Portrait Shows

Work The Bodies   Whole Canvas

Paint It Healthy   Splash In Love

Portrait Shows   Looks Of Desire

To: Good Feelings About You

Footprints

Family Is A Place

Where Love Always Leaves

Footprints

To: Families

Mothers Arms

Essence Of Time   Like The Wind

Plays A Chime

Loving Tones   Peace Full Bones

In Mother's Arms   There Is No Harm

Just Bliss And A Kiss

Of Essence

Pressed Forever On Our Minds

To: Mothers

Always Knows

Love Comes   Life Shows

Mother's Face   Has Quite A Glow

In A Kiss Or A Wish   Love Always Knows

To: Unending Love

Universal Love

Thoughts Of Life

Universal Love

Feels No Shame   Has No Blame

Releases Pain

Thoughts Of Life

God Is Here! There! Every Where!

Ask A Tree   Or A Flea

Comfort And Bliss   What A Kiss

With Angel Flair   Who Needs Hair

To: Our Core

Time To Fiddle

Dry Ocean Party

High Row Glyphs   Pet Row Glyphs

Beauty's Art   Those Rocks Are Smart

Pleasant Past   Who Needs Gas

Create A Tree   Hey May Be   Or

Front Cover Cave   Back Cover Brave

Picture Perfect   A Thousand Signs

Tell The Time

History's Best   When Undressed

Past the Chisel   Time To Fiddle

To: Future Creations

Always And Forever

Mastery Of Perfection

Power Of Love   Is A Glove

Here And Now   Is On The Way

Always And Forever   That's Our Secret Love

So Dance   With Your Father's Delight

-To: Luther Vandross

Natures Find

Present Time World Of Mine

Love Climes   Resistance Binds Energy's Glove

Let's Shove

Present Mind   Into Natures Find

Harmony Floor   Open Door

Spring Lee Water   Without An Altar

Birds Singing Nursery Rhymes

Contrast Moving   Right In Line

Freedom Swinging   All The Time

To: Living In The Present

Rosa's Bright

Parks Sparked   Civil Motion

Troop Lee Fears   Color Squeals

An Alabama Beauty   With Down Home Fruitage

Our Education Light   Rosa's Bright

To: Rosa Parks

Time's Back

Daylight Savings Time   Spring's Back

Comets Swim Laps   Dust Takes Naps

Easy Flow   Planets Know

New Time Tradition   Rock Intuition

Time's Back   That Ageless Sack

Set Your Speed Spaciously

Clock Within Doesn't Spin

Sleeps In Covers   You'll Discover

To: Thoughts Of Time

Flick My Switch

Tree of life   Must Be Nice

Branches Full Of Light

Deceit And Hatred   Run From Sight

Now I'm Thinking   Call Me Bright

Revelations Bold   Stories Old

Pass A Twig   Figs Of Thee

Electric Trunk   Without The Funk

Flick My Switch   Without The Twitch

To: Turning On Your Inner Switch

Forecast's Bright

Spasmodic Motion   Pass The Lotion

Feeling Slow   No Place To Go

Ego's Got A Grin   Funny Thing

He Thinks We're Kin

I Know How   Remember Now

All It Takes   Is love Cakes

Connection Yeast   What A Feast

The Sweet Exciting   Taste Of Mind

The Forecast Light   Is Shining Bright

God Just Said   We're Twins in Grins

To: Segment Intending

Loving Flu

Geo Fusion   Rock Confusion

Earth Is Waving   Time To Turn

The Ice Is Joining   Oceans Herd

Old Secrets Sleeping   Fossil Style

Here's A Towel   Show Us How

Broken Borders   Are Made To Order

Mosaic Soul   Time To Roll

Grout My Spirit   Paint In Lights

Make Me God In Brights

Yes Gospel True   Map's In You

All You Need Is

That

Loving Flu

To: Changing Thoughts

Lost Then Found

Boomer Babies   All The Gravy

Retro Dressing   Heart Full Blessings

Universal Plan   Direct from Baby Land

All The Tools   Before the Schools

We Took The Test   Which Church Is Best

Must Be One   Now Come Guns

Blood Covered Love   Let's Pull The Rug

Lost Then Found   Endless Bounds

Ageless Glove   Universal Love

Full Circle Snug   Take Out The Plugs

Without The Tugs   There Are No Thugs

To: Re-Thinking

Equal

Let Your Emotions

Start With Joy

Then All Things

Are Equal

To: Joy

Unending Life

Unending Life

That Paradise Mile   Holy Style

Death's A Word   Body Heard

A Quantum Leap   You Don't Need Feet

Amazing Feat   From Your Childhood Seat

Now You Know   Life Is Grand

All You See   Is   Yours To Be

Fly Your Kite   Start Tonight

Transforming Light   Is Shining Bright

Ego's Missed Another Flight

To: Eternal Life

Moon Light Shines

Proactive Traction   Dead Sea Action

Spinning Earth   Starts To Squeal

Thoughts of Change   What's My Range

Upper Realm Motion   Certainty Potion

Life Is Well   There Is No Spell

Expansion Grand   You're the Plan

With Lightning Spools   Darkness Cooled

Connection Guest   Joy Is Best

Take A Grip   Do A Flip

Desire Shines   All The Time

In Our Minds

To: Earth's Changes

Transforming Beam

Bread of Shame   Ego's Flame

Bubble And Squeeze   Disembark Please

Lightning Ladder   Sparks That Matter

Sleepy Gene   God-Lee Queen

Awaken My Thoughts Of We

Transforming Beam

We Are One

Now Time Just Begun

Oh What Fun

To: Transformation

Scent Of Love

Will Free Beauty Shines

Within A Light Filled Rose Garden

Divine Scent Of Love

To: Free Will

Conscious Skean

Crystal Clear   Source Is Here

Delicious Jar   Twist Off Cap

Flowing Love   Bottom Less Bliss

Body Kiss Mist   No Matter Platter

Full Fillment Batter   Vibration Horse

Life Filled Source   Cayce's Giving Stream

A Perfect Slice   My Conscious Skean

Found The Beam

To: Attraction

Natures Course

Give Us Water   Give Us Air

Our Heart's Choice   A Wellness Flair

That Law Of Attraction

Contrast Knows   Expansion Glows

Ask Your Wish   Sit In Bliss

17 Clicks Universe Glows   And Starts the Show

Wellness Vibes   Guiding Tide

Mind's Resting   Peace Is Mine

To: Peace Of Mine

Pop The Top

50 Winks And Some Blinks

So Today Is

Creative Workshop Day

In A Sea   Tranquility

Mind Knows The Way

Because

Numbers Wear No Guns   Lottery Says How Fun

Let Your Creative Box   Pop The Top

And Bring Some Light Your Way

To: Aging Thoughts

Clean Slate

Clean Slate   Years Do Mate

Beautiful Dream State   Histories Opening Gate

Birthday Britches   High Heel Glitches

Fun Is One   And Never Done

Rainbows Filled With Gain

Age Has Found A Name

Now's The Aim

Joy's The Game

To: Living Each Day

In Sight

Creative Workshop Day

Is

Deliberate Focus   With Creative Lotion

Energy Motion   Joy Full Potion

You're A

What IS Magnet   With Thoughts Of Attraction

Your Other Eye Mind's

Imaginary Flight   Is Leaving Right On Time

With Multi Vision Might

Touch Me God In Brights   With All The Lights

To: Designing Your Life

All Aboard

Comforts On The Way

That Energy Trip   Gets A Grip

It's A Friendly Train   Motherly Mane

No One's Feeling Pain

The Wellness Gain   Has No Stain

All Aboard

Love Track   Don't Look Back

Straight Ahead

To Fun And Games   Your Choice With God's Voice

It's Your Plan   Bring Your Band

And A Music Stand

To: Road To Better Feelings

Bliss Sleigh

New York Holiday Shopping Spree

And Some Fees

Taxi Says It Best

Original Pan   City's Grand

Hey Money Pole   Fill My Hole

Red And White   God Is Tight

Santa's Crossing   Fifth Tonight

A Yellow Sleigh   Meters Say

Kiss Me   Modern Day

To: New York At Christmas

Music Man

Family Trance Uncles And Aunts

Santa Wears Baggy Pants

Holiday Wishes   Energy Kisses

Love's Our Music Man

To: A Holiday Wish

Alignment's In

Awareness Toast   An Ego Roast

Resistance Free   With New Energy

Dream Mill   Desire's Will

Pure Manifest Treat   At Your Feet

Now Your Creative Pack Is Pure

Energy Map

Simple Way   Like Sleeping In Hay

That Positive Clock Chimes   Alignment's In

You're A Twin

To: Awareness

Better Thoughts

Creative Day   Time to Play

Years And Fears   Step to the Rear

Nows In Time   For A Positive Find

Just Forward Focus   Cells In Motion

The Alignment Chime   Is Ringing In Your Mind

Brace Yourself

For Even Better   Thoughts In Dream Time

You Will Do Your Best   There Is No Test

And God's Your Guest

To: Positive Thinking

Birthday' Dream

An Ageless Dream With

Healthy Choices   And Smiling Voices

Pure Love   Captured In My Mind

Birthday's Singing

Feels Good To Be

Free Again

Time's Undone

God Is   Never Done

To: Birthdays

Pryor's Loving Grand

Pryor Man   had A Plan

That Human Cake's   A Smiling Bake And Shake

Master Wow   Comedy Proud

He Knows How   In A Crowd

Tat Too Vote   A God Lee Tote

Our Perpetual Comedy Stand

Pryor's Loving Grand

To: Richard Pryor

Joy Full Glee

Be Your Wishes

That's Bliss   Without A Twist

Love Power Any Hour

It's Resistance Free   Like The Undead Sea

Our Non Physical Lights   Are Shining Might

With Vibration Cushions That Are Bushing Free

Now I'm Me

Creative Pass Word Is

Abundance In Joy Full Glee

To: Creating

Selective Sifter

Attraction Action   In Abe Head Fashion

A Joy Full Dress   That Exits Stress

With The Original Grin   Light Comes In

A Selective Sifter   Makes Love In Whispers

Oh That Allowance Sister   Is A Vibration Twister

A Projection Intent Listener   With No Blisters

Are You Ready Mister

To: Abraham

Holo Gram Show

Higher Levels   Come Together

In Warp Speed   If You Please

A Brain Bank   In A Sameness Tank

Then A Conformity Peg   Breaks a Leg

Our Hologram Shows

Individuals Glow

Even Here In Tow   So Let's Go

You're The One   To Start The Show

To: Hands Of Light

Morphoric Tides

100 Monkeys   Ain't That Funky

Causative Field   Makes Them Squeal

New Wave   Banana Peels

Odic Force   That Iliaster Course

A Higher Plane

That's The Same

Separate Poles   Fill Their Wholes

Morphoric Tides

Comfort's Riding   On Our Vibes

To: Self-Healing

Connection Toast

Bio Plasma State   Orgone Energy Mate

Neutrino Power   Thoughts That Matter

Dance Of Life   Focus Bright

With Your Deliberate Creation Kite

Segment Intending   Spears Confusion

Now A Ghost   Clarity's The Host

Joy Full   Connection Toast

No Worry   There Is No Roast...

To: Happiness

Pastel Place

Cosmic Life

Our Healing Flight   Is A Plane Of Light

With Network Grace   And Golden Taste

A Pastel Place in Opulent Space

To : Cosmic Life

Take A Seat

Be A Resistance Free   Positive Tree

With Naches Flow   Your World Will Glow

In Heavens Snow

Belief System Knows   You're The Show

Ask And Plan   Desire Man

Then Take A Seat   Rest Those Feet

Mind's Will Leap

And All God Is

Will Grow

To: Faith

Unfocused Illusion

Unfocused Illusions Drift

Into Shadows Of Reality

Trying To Find Our Core

To: Confusion

One Will

The Essence Of Love

Stirs Sparks Of Desire

Blazing Into One Will

To: Unity

Fallen Leaves

Dance Of fallen Leaves

A Haiku Waltz Embracing Air

God Lee Breeze of Death

To: Fall

Empty Wings

Empty Wings Of Anger

Shading Desires With Walls

Fly Away Claws

Now Has Been Found

To: Low Vibrations

Frozen Water

Frozen Water Flow

Moving Quietly Thru My Life

Thaw In Love of Light

To: Blocked Energy

Grand Structure

Beautiful Stream Of Thoughts

Released In The Universe

Create A Grand Structure Of Love

That Heals

To: Positivity

Mystery Strings

Lunar Mystery Strings

Moonlit Rivers Of Love

Strumming For The Lover

To: Rumi

Moonlit Rivers

Moonlit Rivers Of Love

Light Filled Streams Of Your Beauty

Shining In The

Now

To: Self Love

Beauty All The Way

Programmed By Love

A Mining Moment   With Activated Motion

And Achievement Lotions

It's Your Creation   A New Invention

Joy Full   Every Day

Ask A Tree   Deer Maybe

Which Way Is The Light

Program Love   Give Me Hugs

Beauty All The Way

To: Self Esteem

My Wish

May You Be Filled With Joyous Thoughts

That Create Happiness And Love

From Your Source

Comfort And Bliss   Life's Course

A Beauty Wish

Light My Bands

Santa Man   Creation Grand

Vibration Plan   Is Quite A Stand

Those Giving Tours   With Smiles Galore

Pure Energy Lifts   And Universal Gifts

Comfort In Tow   Every Mind's A Glow

Santa Man

Here's My Hand

Light My Bands

To: Santa

Source Kind

Special Day Let Us Pray

Jesus Creation   That Energy Vibration

Your Universal Thought   Is Self Taught

With Cords Of Love   You Light Minds

Anytime

Because You're Plugged Into

Our Source Kind

To: Universal Love

No Shame

Sense Of Purpose   The Expanded Mind

That Well Being Deal   Is Quite a Meal

Good Tastes Better   Even Allowing Pain

It's All The Same

Self-Centered Fame   Has No Shame

Everything Is Your Game

To: Good Feelings

Bird Power

Bird Power Any Hour

Bring A Tale   Or Set Sail

Physical Chirps Of Glee

Grab A Seed   Nest Lee Tree

Feathers Comfort Thee

In Flight   God Lee Might

Angels We Can See

Perfect Harmony

To: Our Birds

Alaska Groans

Perma Frost Cross   Who's The Boss

Ice Melting Rage   Earth's Engaged

Human Clones   Stem Cell Drones

In A Fizz   DNA Quiz

Truth In Stone   Weather Tones

Alaska Groans   Watch For Bones

To: Earth Changes

Metopic Trip

Rotation Change   Film's In Range

An Earthquake Wave   Brings Mili Second Gain

Faster Motion   Bring On The Lotion

Metopic Trip   Metope Mark

Now's The Time For

Some Sparks...

To: Earth's Rotation

Feel The Show

Yearning For Desire   Hearts On Fire

Mili Second Wiz   You're The Kid

Feel The Show   Charkas Know

Emotional Tools   Makes Things Cool

Joy In A Spool   Life   Designed Pool

Healing Power   Of The Hour

To: Your Choices

Cloudless Dreams

Cloudless Dreams Bring

God Given Beams

Artist Hand   Is Beauty's Stand

Simple Wealth   Of Pleasure Found

In The Now

True Love Colors   Fill Each Day

Species Proud

What A Lovely Crowd

To: Living In The Now

Grab a Torch

Humanity's Pain   Is An Energy Drain

A Freedom Stain   Who Knows Sane

With Connection Break   Your Responsibility Aches

In Realities Favor   That's Sick Lee Behavior

Dig Inside   You The Guide

Grab That Torch   Light Your Porch

Starts With You   A Wellness Brew

Mix It Thru   A Smile Or Two

Kiss Your Mirror   Cause You Know

You Life Is More   Than Fingers And Toes

It's Love Gloves   With Joy Shoes

Thoughts Of Friendship's Loving Stew

To: Better Feelings

God Said

I Am All Religions

I Have No Form   But Love

I Am A Mind   Of Clearness

There Is No Fear   To Grow Here

Only Plants Of Oneness

With

Roots Of Kindness   Branches Of Giving

Trunks Of Abundance   Leaves Of Awareness

Fruits Of Wellness

You Can Call Me   Love Anytime

To: God

Chicago Grand

Chicago's Grand   Lou The Man

Gospel Hunch   World Lee Punch

Lady Love Rawls

You Are   Our Blessing And Dressing

To: Lou Rawls

Memory's Will

The Invisible Hand Of Desire

Holds Memory's Will

In Sweet Silent Threads

Of Time

To: Focused Expansion

Cell Of Life

In Each Cell Of Life

Our Core Star Shines Creative light

Making Each Day Bright

To: Us

One To Be

Photo Shoot   Life Is Mute

Dozen Souls   Left The Hole

Angels Brought A Sleigh

Life's Work Pleasure   Coal Behavior

Down Home Flavor

Earth To Dust   Info Rust

Notes Of Trust

Re- Incarnation Time   Light Filled Line

One To Be   All To See

Universe Says It's So

To: Sago Miners

Will Of Love

A World Of No Blame

Sings And Acts As One

Endowed With The Will

Of Love

To: Peace

Healing Gain

The Voice Of Pain

Dies In The Presence Of Love

Positive Thoughts Of Healing Gain

Cover Our Minds And Body

To: Self Love

Love

Power Perfect   Moment Magic

Core Star Patched

 Life Now Hatches   Joy Full Batches

Love Now Matches

To: Harmony

Who Am I

Who Am I

Power Station

 Or

 Disconnected Train   Locked In Pain

I Am

Changing Clay   Creating Days

Desire Crazed   Pleasure Maize

Pure Expression   New Dimension

Love In

Glorious Rage

To: Who We Are

Remember Spark

Remember Spark

Power Plant   Found Some Ants

Injury Turns To Dust   If You Must

Fear Full Thrust   A Thought Form Rust

And Confirmation Bust

Wall Of Self   That Resistance Shelf

It's Separation Craze   The Sinking Haze

With Energy Blocked   You're A Dis-Eased Clock

Your Enlightenment Tool

Is The Self Exploring School

Loving Guest   You're The Best

Time To Feel   The Emotional Wheel

It Steers   You Cheer

Remember Spark   You're The Ark

Today's The Mine   Start In Your Mind

To: Reconnecting With Your Core

Health Food

Concentration Power   Builds A Tower

Harmonic Induction   Is A Body Function

Taste Is Real   A Natural Flowing Deal

Positive Charge   Love Is Large

A Wellness Barge

What A Slice   No Need To Dice

Energy Knows The Plan

Your World Is Grand   That's A Health Food Plan

To: Wellness

Holistic Dance

In Our Other World   Charkas Swirl

Angels Twirl

Upbeat Trance   A Beauty Glance

Life With Love   Is Multi Chance

That Holistic Dance

Make A Note   Health Can Vote

To: Health

Creation Mix

Ocean's Blue   Living Stew

Whales Perceive   Fish Receive

Life Is Long   Tails Are Strong

Forget The Air   Who Needs Hair

We Can Breathe Anywhere

To: Ocean Life

Changing Light

Different Glass   Changing Light

Mirror's Task   Shows You Bright

Freedom's Sight Is Peace Full Might

Comfort Minus Resistance

Day And Night

To: Pure Thought

What A Spark

Self-Love That

Rose Colored Glass   A Delight Full Blast

Is A New Path Task

It's A 100 Proof Win   A 10 Pin Strike

Love Is Speaking Thru A Mike

What A Spark   You're Dancing   In Your Park

Signals Pure   Our Hearts Are Sure

Born Out Of Contrast Tone

Is Our Essence Zone

To: Well Being

Sung By Love

Delicious Water Connected

Life Sustaining Pleasures

Relight A Familiar Desire

Sung By Love

To: Pleasures

Here's To Here

61 Seconds Truth In Question

Not In This Dimension

That Rotation Change   Makes Spinning Years

Look Like Space Of Fears

Visible Motion Call Us   Land Of Oceans

World Of Tears

Here's To Here

To: 2005

Ready To Mine

Vibration Year   Thumbs Up Here

New Birth Learning   Core Thought Yearning

Bird Like Bee   Are Resistance Free

Makes Sense To Me

Sensitive Glee

Back Flip Time   Channel's Open

Ready To Mine

To: A New Way Of Thinking

Core Star Honeymoon

Core Star Honeymoon   Soothing Place

Filled With Grace

Unfolding Self   United Shelves

God Born Elves

Travel Pass   Loving Gas

Expansive Essence Class

Life's Your Task   Shed The Mask

Moment One   Has Begun

To: Living Your Life's Task

A Prayer

Core Star Light Hold Me Tight

Play The Song We Sang That Night

Every Night

Friendship

Friendship Is

A Positive Thought

That Puts A Smile

On Our face

Here's To Grins!

To: Friends

Looking Round

Looking Round   Earth's Got Sound

Wind's A Maestro

Seasoned Band   Dancing Grand

Brad ford's Playing In Pears

Red Bud's Glancing   Dogwood's Prancing

Cherry's Wearing Pink

Blossom City   Needs No Pity

Harmony's Door Fits   Way More Than Four

Looking Round   Heaven's Found

Who Could Ask For More

To: Spring And The Trees

Glance

The Glance Of Friendship

Eyes Open With A Smile

Sharing Beautiful Churns Of Love

To: Peace

Different Colors

Angels Come   In Different Colors

Enjoyable Flavors   Timely Favors

Friend Lee Bunch   Mind Lee Touch

Love Has No Slaves

To: Angels

Country Taste

What A Seat! With Elite

Music Blend   Georgia's Friend

Country Taste   Ray's Got Grace

Love's An Ageless Fan

To: Ray Charles

Shocks Of Time

Tingling Nerves Of Nothing

Touched By Lights Of Peace

Awake From The Shocks Of Time

To: Reconnection

Trees

Let Me Live Here

In The Shadows Of Nothing

Let Me Die Here Too

To: Resistance Free Living

Sound of Air

Hear The Sound Of Air

Moving Thru Empty Branches

Sweet Music Of Love

To: Connection

Daily Garden

The Celebration Of Friends

Pilgrims In Dreams

Frolicking In A Daily Garden

With

Love

To: Life On Earth

Your Name

Many Choices   Different Voices

Source Is Still The Same

Now In One

So Well Done

Saint Is Now Your Name

To: John Paul II

Traceless

God Said

If I AM Above You

Time Is Point Less

If I Am Around You

Time Is Rest Less

If I Am You

Time Is Trace Less

To: Perfect Vibrations

Inner Truth

The Inner Truth Of Life

Censored By Memories Reluctance

Is Found In The Reality

Of The Now

To: Living In the Now

Understanding

Understanding The Law Of Attraction

And

Passing On The Revelation

Is A Noble Life's Endeavor

To: Law Of Attraction

Which Branch

Beauty In The Trees

Active Insects Love To Nest

Which Branch Suits Me Best

To: Life Choices

Well Being Fever

Traveling East   An Energy Feast

Clouds Are Spreading   Lots With Rain

A Natures Dish   Our Mirror's Wish

Well Being Fever

Said A Beaver

Day And Night

Makes Me Bright

Well Being Thoughts   Are Self Taught

To: Natures Energy Sources

Eternal Thoughts

Eternal Thoughts Of Love

Will Glow Rhythmically

In The Lovers

Garden Of Desire

To: Desire

Glow of Spring

The Glow Of Spring

Makes

Seeds Of Love Change In Place

World Of Peace Full Grace

To: Spring

Ribbons Of Energy

Delicious Ribbons Of Energy

Melt Into Glittering Thoughts

Of Love

To: Positive Thoughts

Odorless Taste

Odorless Taste Of Death

Life has Now Begun To Bloom

Thanks To Your Blanket

To: Leaves

Burnished Shades

Burnished Shades Of Intensity

Golden Tattoos Of Desire

Color My Eyes With Love

To: Focus

Bird Of Paradise

Bird Of Paradise

Sitting Gently In Memory

Feathers Covering The Light

Of Truth

Awake!

To: Allowing

Sweet Moment

The Sweet Moment Of Desire

Steps Gently Into Tender Dreams

Of Love

To: Fulfillment

Your Core

Abundance In Life

Appears In Humble Giving

Of Love

From Your Core

To: Abundance

Soul Man Song

Wicked Pickett   What A Ticket

Midnight Hour   Gospel Note

Mustang Sally   Got A Vote

Soul Man Song   Love Is Long

Voice In Mind   Is Singing   All The Time

To: Wilson Pickett

To obtain more copies

Of The 2006 Collection

Our Address Is Shortsleeves.net

or

1116 Harpeth Ridge Drive

Franklin, Tennessee

37069-7054

See you Soon.

About the Author

Hello Everyone!

I send you love from Tennessee!

For those of you who know me And for those who have yet to meet me, I thought you might be interested in how I found my life's path. For 25 years I thought the shoe business was it, but 10 years ago my thoughts started to change. I always was interested in people and had a strong desire to make money, because of my thoughts of lack. The shoe business was the perfect vehicle to do both. Traveling nationwide and working in Asia, Europe and Brazil for years, taught me so many valuable life lessons. I have been blessed with wonderful friends all over the globe. I have been able to create inerasable memories and lasting bonds. Thank you.

Yes, my life was externally comfortable but I still wondered what I was doing. I could not see the point of this me, by what I had been taught, experienced or remembered. The thought of how I appeared to others was more important than self worth. I was plagued with the same situations we all face in one form or another. Addiction to or from something, an inner fear of not being good enough and guilty for not understanding why. Of course the Death word was the ultimate fear for me and everyone around me. I knew all of this was manifesting in various physical forms, weight gain or loss, injuries, health issues and off course not having enough of anything whatever the item desired.

In 1996 my mother died. My world changed. She devoted her life to her family and her religion. Being raised in a devout Irish Catholic home she learned she could love and trust her God as long as she followed the teachings of the church. She believed. I struggled with rules and authority so her path and mine on religion were different. Mom loved her God and prayed that when she died, she would be reconnected with him as well as, all those who had gone before her. I had no idea what to say to God.

I now know her prayers were answered and more but at the time of her death, I felt alone for the first time in my life. It was all about me. She was gone. Who or what but Mother would do what mothers do?

Now separated from her, I was looking for answers I wanted her back. I turned to philosophy beginning with Plato, Aristotle, Heraclitus, Plotinus Lao-Tzu, Nagarjuna, Buddha, Confucius, Augustine. I started studying psychology and noticed anytime the author wanted to project a thought they would use poetry. I never had an interest in poetry, I didn't own a book of poetry.

One poet continued to be quoted in the books I studied. His name is Jalaluddin Rumi, better known as Rumi, who lived in Turkey in the mid-1200's. His family were scholars and theologians of their time. His words seem to call me, so I bought my first poetry book.

His writings completely took over my thoughts. Reading his work I knew my life would never be the same again. It was in reading Rumi's words and his unending search for Shams of Tabriz, that I felt Mothers closeness and connection.

Then I Discovered Rilke, Blake, Goethe, Dante, Dickinson Takahashi, John Paul II and other eastern and western poets.

In all of these friends, I found the same message regardless of the time portal: That love of self, reconnecting with your spirit, brings love to All. In order to love and to give the gift, I first had to be the vessel that held love for all things. With love there is no death, only eternal life. Our loved ones live and always will.

Our inner voices connected in one.

This is the kind of message I've heard all my life, but it was Moms complete connection with God that opened a door for me thru poetry. I looked and all I needed to do was enter. I had to forgive myself so I could forgive others. I was looking to others for help, before I helped myself. The answers were within me.

I create the world I live in, either with spirit or without.
Without is no longer an option.
Well-Being is our gift to ourselves thru our spirits.
I am never alone living in spirit. No one is.

My first book of poetry, Short Sleeves A Book For Friends, was self published in 2003 and was a work based on special occasions poems to family and friends. It was hand written and put together by local printer, Mr. Charles Terrell and his assistants Marion and Portia

My new book : Shortsleeves A Book For Friends, 2006 Collection is being released this month, on shortsleeves.net for $11.95, free shipping. It can also be found in stores: ISBN# 0-9778130-0-2

Within this work are poems for everyone, regardless of age, and the time they are read. These thoughts of love and an eternal life of joy are written for you, in your now, if you allow it. It's never to late and you never get it wrong. And you can simply start with a smile while looking in the mirror. You know your truth.

 In this book are thoughts you already know. Why buy a book about stuff you already know? Because it's your gift of love, that's worth repeating and sharing. We don't need to leave our physical bodies to enjoy us, to connect to our source.

Just start loving yourself in spirit NOW, and things begin to change. Everything looks different in a glorious way.

You make a difference, and there is great love waiting for you now!

Hope to see you soon!

To contact me: hal@shortsleeves.net
I would love to hear from you.
With Joy,
Hal Manogue

Printed in the United States
49619LVS00001B/208-249

9 780977 813001